# TREES

AURUM PRESS

**W**hat does he plant who plants a tree?
   He plants the friend of sun and sky;
He plants the flag of breezes free;
The shaft of beauty, towering high;
He plants a home to heaven anigh
For song and mother-croon of bird
In hushed and happy twilight heard —
The treble of heaven's harmony —
These things he plants who plants a tree.

    HENRY CUYLER BUNNER, *THE HEART OF THE TREE*

The poplars are felled, farewell to the shade,
   And the whispering sound of the cool colonnade;
The winds play no longer and sing in the leaves,
Nor Ouse on his bosom their image receives.

Twelve years have elapsed, since I last took a view
Of my favourite field, and the bank where they grew;
And now in the grass behold they are laid,
And the tree is my seat, that once lent me a shade.

The blackbird has fled to another retreat,
Where the hazels afford him a screen from the heat,
And the scene, where his melody charmed me before,
Resounds with his sweet-flowing ditty no more.

Tis a sight to engage me if any thing can,
To muse on the perishing pleasures of man;
Though his life be a dream, his enjoyments, I see,
Have a being less durable even than he.

WILLIAM COWPER, *THE POPLAR FIELD*

Huge Elm thy rifted trunk all notched and scarred
   Like to a warrior's destiny – I love
To stretch me often on such shadowed sward
And hear the sighs of summer leaves above
Or on thy buttressed roots to sit and lean
In careless attitude and there reflect
On times and deeds and darings that have been
Old cast aways now swallowed in neglect
While thou art towering in thy strength of heart
Stirring the soul to vain imaginings
In which life's sordid being hath no part
The wind in that eternal ditty sings
Humming of future things that burns the mind
To leave some fragment of itself behind.

JOHN CLARE, *SALTER'S TREE*

Loveliest of trees, the cherry now
   Is hung with bloom along the bough,
And stands about the woodland ride
Wearing white for Eastertide.

Now, of my threescore years and ten,
Twenty will not come again,
And take from seventy springs a score,
It only leaves me fifty more.

And since to look at things in bloom
Fifty springs are little room,
About the woodlands I will go
To see the cherry hung with snow.

        A. E. HOUSMAN, *A SHROPSHIRE LAD*

Much can they praise the trees so straight and high,
The sailing pine, the cedar proud and tall,
The vine-prop elm, the poplar never dry,
The builder oak, sole king of forests all,
The aspin good for staves, the cypress funeral,
The laurel, meed of mighty conquerors
And poets sage, the fir that weepest still,
The yew obedient to the bender's will,
The birch for shafts, the sallow for the mill,
The myrrh sweet-bleeding in the bitter wound,
The warlike beech, the ash for nothing ill,
The fruitful olive, and the platane round,
The carver holm, the maple seldom inward sound.

EDMUND SPENSER, *FAERIE QUEENE*

We had set up camp beside the only tree for miles, and a cricket was singing somewhere deep within its thorny branches. Apart from that noise and the sputtering of the flames, the world was soundless, without even a wisp of wind; it seethed with silence. Apart from the slow, ponderous shuffle of the hobbled beasts, it was entirely still. In this stillness, I could see, lay the fruitfulness of the desert that mystics had found across many ages. It calmed the soul and made it possible to fix the attention at any point one chose without distraction. I wished, that evening, I could remain in that spot, motionless, until I had so absorbed the desert's balm that something unknown to me dawned upon my understanding. Lying there at peace, one felt so close to a brink of revelation that it seemed almost within willpower. But not quite. Not on this journey.

GEOFFREY MOORHOUSE, *THE FEARFUL VOID*

**B**y the lakes that thus outspread
   Their lone waters, lone and dead,
Their sad waters, sad and chilly
With the snows of the lolling lily,
By the mountains – near the river
Murmuring lowly, murmuring ever,
By the grey woods, – by the swamp
Where the toad and newt encamp,
By the dismal tarns and pools
   Where dwell the Ghouls,
By each spot the most unholy,
By each nook most melancholy,
There the traveller meets, aghast,
Sheeted Memories of the Past,
Shrouded forms that start and sigh
As they pass the wanderer by,
White-robed forms of friends long given,
In agony, to the Earth – and Heaven.

EDGAR ALLAN POE, *DREAMLAND*

This is the forest primeval. The murmuring pines and the hemlocks,
  Bearded with moss, and in garments green, indistinct in the twilight,
Stand like Druids of old, with voices sad and prophetic,
Stand like harpers hoar, with beards that rest on their bosoms.
Loud from its rocky caverns, the deep-voiced neighbouring ocean
Speaks, and in accents disconsolate answers the wail of the forest.

This is the forest primeval; but where are the hearts that beneath it
Leaped like the roe, when he hears in the woodland the voice of the huntsman?
Where is the thatch-roofed village, the home of Acadian farmers,
Men whose lives glided on like rivers that water the woodlands,
Darkened by shadows of earth, but reflecting an image of heaven?
Waste are those pleasant farms, and the farmers for ever departed!
Scattered like dust and leaves, when the mighty blasts of October
Seize them, and whirl them aloft, and sprinkle them far o'er the ocean;
Naught but tradition remains of the beautiful village of Grand-Pré.

HENRY WADSWORTH LONGFELLOW, *A TALE OF ACADIE*

When the long, varnished buds of beech
    Point out beyond their reach,
And tanned by summer suns
Leaves of black bryony turn bronze,
And gossamer floats bright and wet
From trees that are their own sunset,
Spring, summer, autumn I come here,
And what is there to fear?
And yet I never lose the feeling
That someone else behind is stealing
Or else in front has disappeared;
Though nothing I have seen or heard,
The fear of what I might have met
Makes me still walk beneath these boughs
With cautious step as in a haunted house.

ANDREW YOUNG, *THE BEECHWOOD*

**H**ow innocent were these
   Trees, that in mist-green May,
Blown by a prospering breeze,
Stood garlanded and gay;
Who now in sundown glow
Of serious colour clad
Confront me with their show
As though resigned and sad.

Trees who unwhispering stand
Umber and bronze and gold,
Pavilioning the land
For one grown tired and old;
Elm, chestnut, beech and lime,
I am merged in you, who tell
Once more in tones of time
Your foliaged farewell.

SIEGFRIED SASSOON, *OCTOBER TREES*

Peace to these little broken leaves,
    That strew our common ground;
That chase their tails, like silly dogs,
    As they go round and round.
For though in winter boughs are bare,
    Let us not once forget
Their summer glory, when these leaves
    Caught the great Sun in their strong net;
And made him, in the lower air,
    Tremble – no bigger than a star!

W. H. DAVIES, *LEAVES*

The brilliant light of day fell through the irregular opening in the high branches of the trees and streamed down, softened amongst the shadows of big trunks. Here and there a narrow sunbeam touched the rugged bark of a tree with a golden splash, sparkled on the leaping water of the brook, or rested on a leaf that stood out, shimmering and distinct, on the monotonous background of sombre green tints. The clear gap of blue above his head was crossed by the quick flight of white rice-birds whose wings flashed in the sunlight, while through it the heat poured down from the sky, clung about the steaming earth, rolled among the trees, and wrapped up Willems in the soft and odorous folds of air heavy with the faint scent of blossoms and with the acrid smell of decaying life. And in that atmosphere of Nature's workshop Willems felt soothed and lulled into forgetfulness of his past, into indifference as to his future. The recollection of his triumphs, of his wrongs and of his ambition vanished in that warmth, which seemed to melt all regrets, all hope, all anger, all strength out of his heart.

JOSEPH CONRAD, *AN OUTCAST OF THE ISLANDS*

Let my soul, a shining tree,
   Silver branches lift towards thee,
Where on a hallowed winter's night
The clear-eyed angels may alight.

And if there should be tempests in
My spirit, let them surge like din
Of noble melodies at war;
With fervour of such blades of triumph as are
Flashed in white orisons of saints who go
On shafts of glory to the ecstasies they know.

SIEGFRIED SASSOON, *TREE AND SKY*

We are accustomed to consider Winter the grave of the year, but it is not so in reality. In the stripped trees, the mute birds, the disconsolate gardens, the frosty ground, there is only an apparent cessation of Nature's activities. Winter is a pause in music, but during the pause the musicians are privately tuning their strings, to prepare for the coming outburst. When the curtain falls on one piece at the theatre, the people are busy behind the scenes making arrangements for that which is to follow. Winter is such a pause, such a fall of the curtain. Underground, beneath snow and frost, next spring and summer are secretly getting ready. The rose which young ladies will gather six months hence for hair or bosom, are already in hand. In Nature there is no such thing as paralysis. Each thing flows into the other, as movement into movement in graceful dances; Nature's colours blend in imperceptible gradation; all her notes are sequacious.

ALEXANDER SMITH, *LAST LEAVES*

**A**y me! ay me! the woods decay and fall,
　The vapours weep their burthen to the ground,
Man comes and tills the earth and lies beneath,
And after many a summer dies the swan.
Me only cruel immortality
Consumes: I wither slowly in thine arms, here at the quiet limit
Here at the quiet limit of the world,
A white-haired shadow roaming like a dream
The ever silent spaces of the East,
Far-folded mists, and gleaming halls of morn.

ALFRED LORD TENNYSON, *TITHONUS*

First published 1989 by Aurum Press Ltd
33 Museum Street, London WC1A 1LD

Conceived, edited and designed by Russell Ash & Bernard Higton
Copyright © 1989 by Russell Ash & Bernard Higton

All rights reserved. No part of this book may be reproduced
or utilized in any form or by any means, electronic or
mechanical, including photocopying, recording or by any
information storage or retrieval system, without permission
in writing from Aurum Press Ltd.

A CIP catalogue record for this book is available from
the British Library

ISBN 1 85410 074 2

Printed in Hong Kong by Imago

Photographs in order of appearance: Julian Nieman/Susan Griggs Agency; Mark E. Gibson; John Sims; Frank Horvat; Horst Munzig/Susan Griggs Agency; G & J Images/Image Bank; Geoff Renner/Robert Harding Picture Library; Larry Ulrich; Tony Evans; Adam Woolfitt/Susan Griggs Agency; Ross M. Horowitz/Image Bank; John Sims; Larry Ulrich; Larry Ulrich; John Sims; C. Caket/ZEFA.

Text extracts from the following sources are reprinted with the permission of their publishers: Geoffrey Moorhouse, *The Fearful Void*, Hodder & Stoughton, 1974; Siegfried Sassoon, 'Tree and Sky' and 'October Trees', from *Collected Poems*, Faber & Faber, 1961; Andrew Young, 'The Beechwood', from *Collected Poems*, Jonathan Cape, 1950; W.H. Davies, 'Leaves', from *Collected Poems*, Jonathan Cape, 1942.